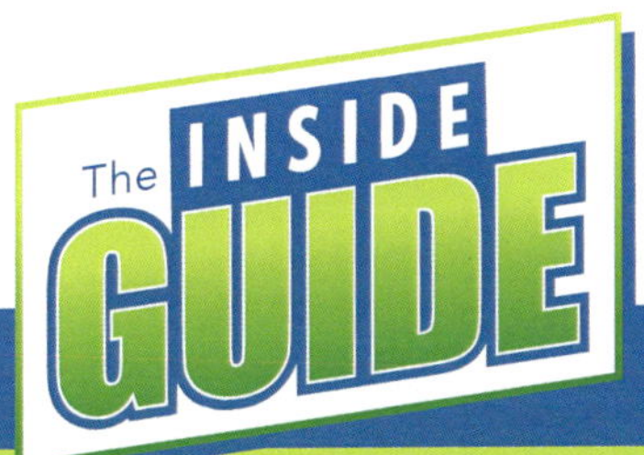

CIVIL RIGHTS HEROES

Rosa Parks

By Amy B. Rogers

New York

Published in 2022 by Cavendish Square Publishing, LLC
29 E. 21st Street, New York, NY 10010

First Edition

Website: cavendishsq.com

Portions of this work were originally authored by Barbara M. Linde and published as *Rosa Parks* (*Civil Rights Crusaders*). All new material this edition authored by Amy B. Rogers.

Library of Congress Cataloging-in-Publication Data

Names: Rogers, Amy B., author.
Title: Rosa Parks / Amy B. Rogers.
Description: New York : Cavendish Square Publishing, [2022] | Series: The inside guide: Civil Rights heroes | Includes bibliographical rreferences and index.
Identifiers: LCCN 2020028958 | ISBN 9781502660169 (library binding) | ISBN 9781502660145 (paperback) | ISBN 9781502660152 (set) | ISBN 9781502660176 (ebook)
Subjects: LCSH: Parks, Rosa, 1913-2005–Juvenile literature. | African American civil rights workers–Alabama–Montgomery–Biography–Juvenile literature. | African American women civil rights workers–Alabama–Montgomery–Biography–Juvenile literature. | Civil rights–United States–History–Juvenile literature. | Montgomery (Ala.)–Biography–Juvenile literature.
Classification: LCC F334.M753 P38635 2022 | DDC 323.092 [B]–dc23
LC record available at https://lccn.loc.gov/2020028958

Editor: Katie Kawa
Copy Editor: Abby Young
Designer: Andrea Davison-Bartolotta

The photographs in this book are used by permission and through the courtesy of: Cover Universal History Archive/UIG via Getty Images; pp. 4, 12 Bettmann/Getty Images; pp. 6, 9 Courtesy of the Library of Congress; p. 7 PhotoQuest/Getty Images; p. 8 Justin Sullivan/Getty Images; pp. 10, 13 Matt McClain/The Washington Post via Getty Images; p. 14 Stormi Greener/Star Tribune via Getty Images; p. 15 Library of Congress/Corbis/VCG via Getty Images; p. 16 Universal History Archive/Getty Images; p. 18 Underwood Archives/Getty Images; pp. 19, 20, 28 (top left) Don Cravens/The LIFE Images Collection via Getty Images/Getty Images; p. 21 Wikimedia Commons/File:Claudette Colvin.jpg/The Visibility Project/Claudette Colvin/PD; p. 22 William Philpott/Getty Images; p. 24 Monica Morgan/WireImage/Getty Images; p. 25 Kristy Sparow/Getty Images; p. 26 Brendan Smialowski/AFP via Getty Images; p. 27 (top) United States Postal Service via Getty Images; p. 27 (bottom) Mandel Ngan/AFP via Getty Images; p. 28 (bottom left) Bill Pugliano/Getty Images; p. 28 (top right) The Print Collector/Print Collector/Getty Images; p. 28 (bottom right) Joe Raedle/Getty Images; p. 29 (top) Wally McNamee/Corbis Historical/Getty Images; p. 29 (bottom) Gino Santa Maria/Shutterstock.com.

CPSIA compliance information: Batch #CS22CSQ: For further information contact Cavendish Square Publishing LLC, New York, New York, at 1-877-980-4450.

Printed in the United States of America

CONTENTS

Rosa Parks is sometimes called the mother of the civil rights movement.

THE MOTHER OF THE MOVEMENT

Sometimes, one choice can change the world. Rosa Parks proved this when she refused to give up her seat on a bus in Montgomery, Alabama, to a white man. This small act of **rebellion** in 1955 led to big changes. It was the spark that set the civil rights movement on fire across the United States.

Segregation in the South

Today, anyone can sit anywhere they want on a bus. However, that wasn't always the case. Until the 1960s, segregation was legal in many parts of the United States, especially in the South. Segregation was the forced separation of Black and white Americans.

Because of segregation laws, Black Americans had to use separate water fountains, restaurants, and schools. They also could only sit in certain places on city buses, and they had to give up their seats if white passengers wanted them. If they didn't do this, they were arrested. That's what happened to Rosa.

The schools, bathrooms, waiting rooms, and other facilities for Black Americans were often not as nice as the facilities for white Americans.

The Civil Rights Movement

Rosa's refusal to give up her seat on the bus helped bring more attention to the growing civil rights movement. This was a movement led by Black Americans to end legal segregation, fight for basic rights such as the right to vote, and work toward equality. Black Americans had been pushing for these things for many years, but it was during the 1950s and 1960s that this movement became more organized and earned national attention.

One of the most important leaders of the civil rights movement was Dr. Martin Luther King Jr. He first became famous for planning the organized response to Rosa's arrest in Montgomery.

The civil rights movement was a mostly nonviolent, or peaceful, movement.

Beyond the Bus

Although most people only know Rosa because of her actions on the bus that day in Montgomery, that was far from her only accomplishment. After a childhood surrounded by segregation, she became active in the fight for civil rights as she grew up.

Rosa also continued to play a part in the civil rights movement long after she left Montgomery. She became a leader in her church

Fast Fact

TIME magazine named Rosa one of the 100 most influential people of the 20th century.

and her community, eventually working with young people to help them build a better future. She may have been most famous for what happened in 1955, but she spent her entire life trying to help others.

A Role Model of Resistance

Rosa Parks is one of the most famous female members of the civil rights movement. In fact, she was officially named the "Mother of the Modern Day Civil Rights Movement in America" by the U.S. Congress. Today, she's still a **role model** for many people because of her bravery and her desire to do what was right—even when she knew it would get her in trouble.

Although Rosa died in 2005, her **legacy** lives on. Her story is a reminder of the important part Black women played in the civil rights movement and throughout U.S. history.

Rosa's story has inspired many people to believe that one person really can make a difference in the world around them.

Fast Fact

The Rosa Parks Museum is located in Montgomery. The museum is a place where people can learn more about her life and how her actions affected the civil rights movement.

WOMEN IN THE MOVEMENT

Rosa was one of many women who had **roles** in the civil rights movement. However, because they often worked behind the scenes, they didn't become as famous as male leaders, such as Martin Luther King Jr.

Martin's wife, Coretta Scott King, worked alongside her husband and helped keep his legacy alive after his death. Septima Poinsette Clark organized educational workshops to help Black Americans learn to read and write, as well as understand their basic rights. Many other women helped organize marches, took part in protests, and did the hard work that kept the movement moving forward.

Septima Poinsette Clark (*left*) taught Rosa Parks at one of her workshops. Septima became a kind of **mentor** to Rosa.

Shown here is a photo of Rosa's childhood home. It's from a collection of pictures and writings from her life kept by the Library of Congress in Washington, D.C.

EDUCATION AND ACTIVISM

Rosa was no stranger to segregation. Growing up in the South, it was part of her everyday life. Her early life experiences helped shape her future activism in important ways. Rosa was always a person who worked hard to help others.

Young Rosa's Life

Rosa Louise McCauley was born on February 4, 1913, in Tuskegee, Alabama. As a child, Rosa lived with her mother, younger brother, and grandparents in the small Alabama town of Pine Level. Her grandparents had been enslaved before slavery was officially banned by an amendment, or change, to the U.S. Constitution in 1865.

Rosa grew up going to segregated schools and dealing with racism all around her. However, her family taught her the importance of standing up for herself. Rosa worked hard in school. She knew her education was important.

Fast Fact

Racism is the belief that one race is better than others. It also describes the political and social systems that allow one race to be treated better than other races. In the United States, white people have the power in these systems.

SEGREGATED SCHOOLS

The schools Rosa attended, like most schools in the South, were segregated. The schools for Black children often didn't have new books, and some schools didn't even have desks for the students. Segregated schools could exist, according to the U.S. government, as long as the schools for Black children and white children were equal in quality. However, it was clear that this wasn't the reality in the South.

In 1954, the U.S. Supreme Court finally ruled that segregated schools were unconstitutional. This means they went against the U.S. Constitution and could no longer legally exist.

The Supreme Court ruled in the case *Brown v. Board of Education of Topeka* that separate schools could never be truly equal. This case was a major victory in the fight against legal segregation.

Leaving School

Rosa eventually started high school. Her school was connected with Alabama State Teachers College, and she continued to enjoy learning. However, hard times soon hit her family. First, her grandmother got sick. Rosa had to leave school to help her family during her grandmother's illness and after she passed away.

Then, when Rosa was getting ready to return to school, her mother got sick. Rosa was unable to continue her education because she had to help her mother while her brother worked. Rosa later got a job as a seamstress, or a woman who sews, in Montgomery.

When Rosa was younger, she had to put her family before her education.

A Supportive Husband

In 1932, Rosa married Raymond Parks. Raymond worked as a barber and was active in the fight for civil rights. He belonged to the National Association for the Advancement of Colored People (NAACP). This group had already been around for many years by the time Rosa and Raymond were married. It was created to fight for justice and the rights of Black Americans.

Raymond encouraged Rosa to go back to school. With his support, Rosa finished high school. It was often hard for Black Americans at this time to finish high school, but with her husband's help, Rosa did it.

Fast Fact

Rosa and Raymond never had any children.

Raymond understood how important education was, especially to Rosa. It remained important to her throughout her life, and she often encouraged young students, such as the ones shown here with her, to keep learning.

Rosa and the NAACP

Rosa joined her husband as a member of the NAACP in 1943. She once said that the work she did with the NAACP was to "let it be known that we did not wish to continue being **second-class** citizens." She knew this was important work, even though it was also **dangerous**. Members of the NAACP were targeted by racist white people, including members of the police.

Rosa worked as the secretary to the president of the Montgomery branch of the NAACP. She also worked with the young people of this organization. As time went on, her role in the fight for civil rights continued to grow.

Fast Fact

Rosa was also active in the Montgomery Voters League. This was an organization that helped Black people register to vote and prepare for the test they had to take to register. White people weren't given a test, which shows how unfair the voting laws were during this time.

Rosa helped plan meetings of young members of the NAACP, such as the young men and women shown here.

Rosa was arrested when she refused to give up her bus seat to a white man. This is the photo taken at the police station after her arrest.

"TIRED OF GIVING IN"

When people tell the story of Rosa's refusal to give up her bus seat, they often say she didn't want to get up because she was tired. However, Rosa said, "I was not tired physically, or no more tired than I usually was at the end of a working day … No, the only tired I was, was tired of giving in." By 1955, Rosa had grown tired of how Black people were being treated in Montgomery, and she wasn't the only person who felt this way.

The Day That Changed Everything

On December 1, 1955, Rosa left her job as a seamstress in a Montgomery department store after a long day of working hard. She got on a city bus and sat down in the middle section. Black people were only allowed to sit there and in the back of the bus.

At the next stop, the driver told Rosa and three other Black riders to give up their seats for a white man

Fast Fact

In 1943, a bus driver ordered Rosa off a bus because she got on at the front of the bus instead of the back like she was supposed to. He was the same driver who had her arrested in 1955.

because the section for white people was full. Rosa refused. The bus driver had her arrested, and the police took Rosa to jail.

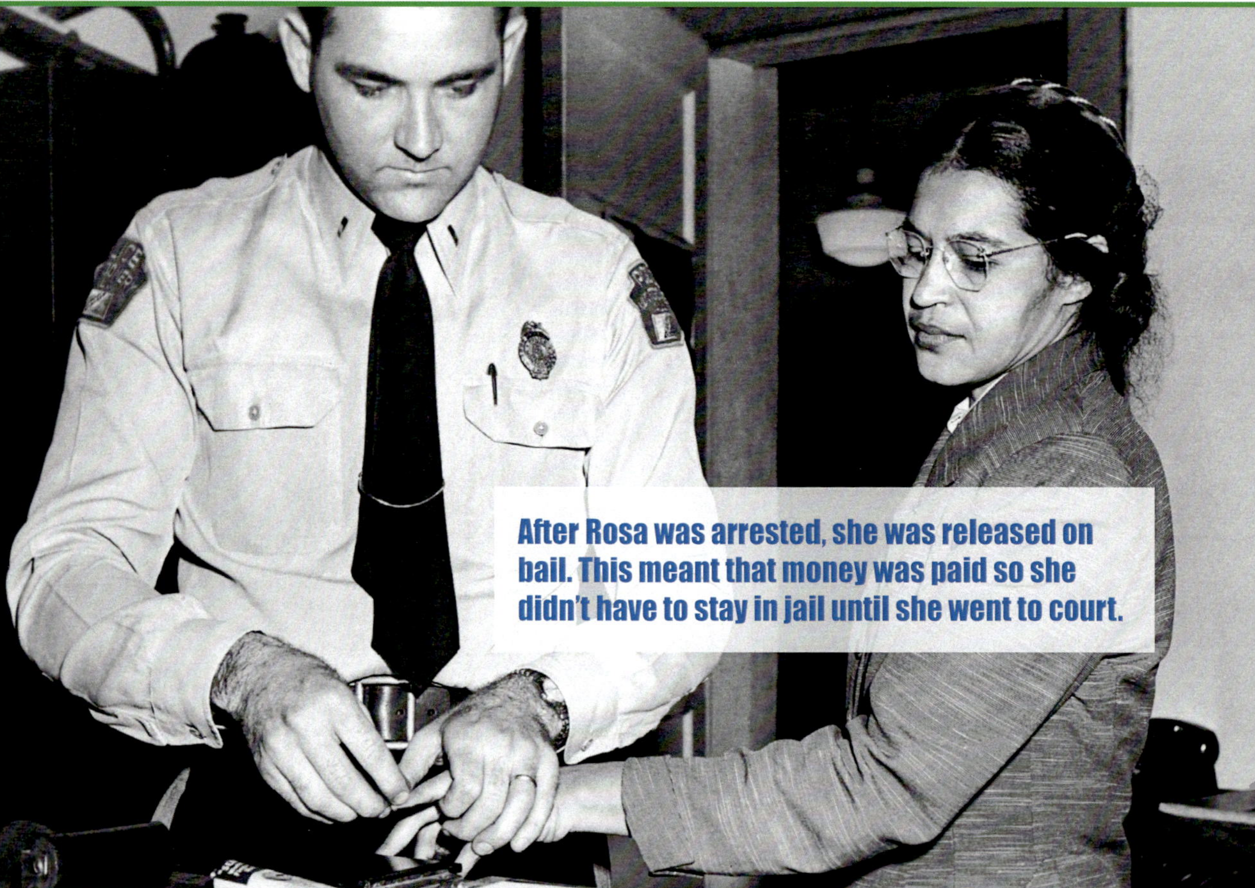

After Rosa was arrested, she was released on bail. This meant that money was paid so she didn't have to stay in jail until she went to court.

The Montgomery Bus Boycott

Rosa's actions inspired Black men and women around Montgomery. They gathered together to plan a **boycott** of the city's buses. Black people were encouraged to avoid taking city buses to protest the unfair segregation law that had led to Rosa's arrest. This would cause the city's bus system to lose a lot of money.

The Montgomery Improvement Association (MIA) was put in charge of the boycott. Its efforts were led by a young preacher named Martin Luther King Jr. This was the first time Martin stepped into the spotlight as an activist, but it wouldn't be the last.

Martin Luther King Jr. can be seen here talking to fellow activists in Montgomery as they planned the bus boycott. Rosa is in the center of the front row of listeners.

Fast Fact

Rosa's refusal to give up her seat was an example of civil disobedience, or the refusal to follow a law that people think is unjust. Civil disobedience is a kind of nonviolent protest.

Changing the Law

The Montgomery bus boycott began on December 5, 1955. This was the day of Rosa's trial. She was found guilty but was fined rather than sent to jail. Her lawyer then filed an appeal, which meant that a higher court would hear her case and possibly make a different ruling.

While Rosa's case was tied up in the court system, the U.S. Supreme Court heard another case about the segregation of public **transportation** in Montgomery. On November 13, 1956, the Supreme Court agreed with a lower court's ruling that the segregation of buses in Montgomery was unconstitutional.

Success in Montgomery

The Montgomery bus boycott was a huge success. It lasted 381 days. It was able to go on for so long because people like Rosa worked hard to make sure Black men and women had different ways to get to work and other places they needed to go. They organized a ride-sharing system using around 200 cars. Other Black people in Montgomery chose to walk or ride bikes.

The boycott gained national attention. It became known as the moment the civil rights movement truly began to grow in the United States. Rosa had started a kind of revolution!

Fast Fact

More than 90 percent of the African Americans in Montgomery took part in the bus boycott.

After the success of the boycott and the Supreme Court's ruling, Rosa could sit anywhere she wanted to on the bus.

CLAUDETTE COLVIN

Rosa Parks is the most famous example of a Black woman who refused to give up her seat on a segregated bus. However, she's far from the only example. In fact, Claudette Colvin was arrested in Montgomery for the same thing months before Rosa. On March 2, 1955, Claudette refused to give up her seat and had to be pulled off the bus by police officers. She was only 15 years old, but she was put in jail. Claudette and three other women were part of the lawsuit that eventually reached the Supreme Court and ended the legal segregation of Montgomery's buses.

Claudette Colvin has stated that Rosa Parks became more famous for her act of civil disobedience because she was older and had more support from the NAACP. However, Claudette's story is also important, and she still shares her story with others today.

Rosa didn't stay in the spotlight after the Montgomery bus boycott, but that doesn't mean she stopped helping people.

LIFE AFTER MONTGOMERY

Rosa's actions were the catalyst, or driving force, behind the first major organized protest of the modern civil rights movement. This made her a hero to many Black Americans but also angered many white Americans. She had to leave her home state, but she never stopped doing her part to make the world a better place.

A New Start

Life in Montgomery wasn't easy for Rosa after her arrest and the protests it sparked. She lost her job, and she had to deal with death threats. She and Raymond left Alabama and eventually settled in Detroit, Michigan.

In Detroit, Rosa worked for an African American congressman named John Conyers. She also served as a deaconess, which is a high position, in the African Methodist Episcopal Church. In 1987, Rosa and her friend Elaine Steele founded the Rosa and Raymond Parks Institute for Self Development. It helps young people stay in school and make a difference in their communities.

High Honors

Rosa's role in the civil rights movement earned her the respect of people around the world. It also earned her many awards and honors during her lifetime. In 1996, President Bill Clinton presented her with the Presidential Medal of Freedom. This is the highest honor a president can give to a **civilian**.

In 1999, the U.S. government honored Rosa again. She was given the Congressional Gold Medal—the highest honor Congress can give to a civilian. This award was given to her to recognize her role as the "First Lady of the civil rights movement."

Fast Fact

The Rosa and Raymond Parks Institute for Self Development hosts a summer program called Pathways to Freedom. It teaches students about the struggle to escape from slavery and the fight for civil rights.

Rosa met with many famous world leaders during her lifetime. She's shown here with Hillary Clinton when Hillary was First Lady of the United States.

Books, Movies, and Barbies

Rosa continued to speak and write about her role in the civil rights movement for the rest of her life. In 1992, her autobiography, or life story, was published. It's titled *Rosa Parks: My Story*. A few years later, she published another book, *Quiet Strength*, which is about her life too.

Rosa's life has also been the subject of a movie. In 2002, *The Rosa Parks Story* was shown on television. It starred Angela Bassett.

Rosa was even the inspiration behind a Barbie doll! In 2019, the Rosa Parks doll was released as a part of a series of Barbie dolls based on women who've done inspiring things.

The Rosa Parks Barbie doll shows that she's still seen as a role model for young people today.

Remembering Rosa

Rosa Parks died on October 24, 2005. Her **casket** was placed in the U.S. Capitol building in Washington, D.C., on October 30, 2005. She was the first woman and the second Black American to

A PLACE IN THE CAPITOL

On February 27, 2013, President Barack Obama spoke to a group gathered in the National Statuary Hall of the U.S. Capitol. This part of the Capitol features statues of famous Americans, and that day, a statue of Rosa Parks officially took its place among them.

President Obama—the first African American U.S. president—honored Rosa as part of a special group of Americans "who've shaped this nation's course." He said, "In a single moment, with the simplest of gestures, she helped change America—and change the world."

President Barack Obama is shown here with the statue of Rosa Parks that can be seen in the National Statuary Hall.

be honored this way. This is an honor usually reserved for U.S. government officials. Around 50,000 people came to the Capitol to pay their last respects to Rosa.

Fast Fact

On February 4, 2013, a special Rosa Parks stamp was released. This stamp was created to celebrate Rosa's life on what would have been her 100th birthday.

Rosa once said, "I am leaving this legacy to all of you ... to bring peace, justice, equality, love and a **fulfillment** of what our lives should be." It's the job of the next generation to carry on her legacy of strength and bravery.

Rosa Parks was an American hero who made her country better by standing up for what she believed was right. After her death, she was honored as a hero in the U.S. Capitol.

TIMELINE

In Rosa's Life	In the World
1913 Rosa Louise McCauley is born on February 4.	**1914–1918** World War I is fought.
	1929 The U.S. stock market crashes, beginning the Great Depression.
	1939–1945 World War II is fought.
1943 Rosa joins the NAACP in Montgomery, Alabama.	
1955 Rosa refuses to give up her seat on the bus on December 1. The Montgomery bus boycott begins on December 5.	
	1963 Martin Luther King Jr. delivers his "I Have a Dream" speech.
1987 Rosa helps found the Rosa and Raymond Parks Institute for Self Development.	
2005 Rosa dies on October 24.	
	2008 Barack Obama becomes the first African American to be elected president of the United States.

THINK ABOUT IT!

1. Why do you think the stories of women in the civil rights movement often aren't as well known as the stories of men in the movement?

2. Why did Rosa start working with the NAACP, even though she knew it could be dangerous?

3. Why do you think Black leaders in Montgomery reacted more strongly to Rosa's arrest than they did to Claudette Colvin's?

4. What can you do to keep the legacy of Rosa Parks alive today?

GLOSSARY

boycott: The act of joining with others in refusing to deal with someone or support a business as a form of protest.

casket: A box or case that holds a dead body so it can be buried properly.

civilian: A person not on active duty in the military.

dangerous: Not safe.

fulfillment: The act of achieving something or making something true or real.

legacy: The lasting effect of a person or thing.

mentor: A person who teaches, gives guidance, or gives advice to someone, especially a less experienced person.

rebellion: Open fighting against authority.

role: A part, job, or function.

role model: A person whom others look up to.

second-class: Not given the same rights or treatment as the rest of the people in a society.

transportation: The act of moving people or things from one place to another.

FIND OUT MORE

Books

Adams, Julia. *Activists and Leaders*. New York, NY: Gareth Stevens Publishing, 2020.

McCormick, Anita Louise. *Rosa Parks and the Montgomery Bus Boycott*. New York, NY: Rosen Publishing, 2018.

Susienka, Kristen. *Rosa Parks*. New York, NY: PowerKids Press, 2020.

Websites

***National Geographic Kids*: Rosa Parks**
kids.nationalgeographic.com/explore/history/african-american-heroes/rosa-parks/
This website features facts and photos from the life of Rosa Parks.

Rosa Parks Museum
www.troy.edu/student-life-resources/arts-culture/rosa-parks-museum/index.html
To learn about or to plan a trip to the Rosa Parks Museum, check out its official website.

***TIME for Kids*: "Riding into History"**
www.timeforkids.com/k1/riding-into-history/
Visit this website to read an informative article about Rosa Parks and see pictures from her life.

Publisher's note to educators and parents: Our editors have carefully reviewed these websites to ensure that they are suitable for students. Many websites change frequently, however, and we cannot guarantee that a site's future contents will continue to meet our high standards of quality and educational value. Be advised that students should be closely supervised whenever they access the Internet.

INDEX